Drugs

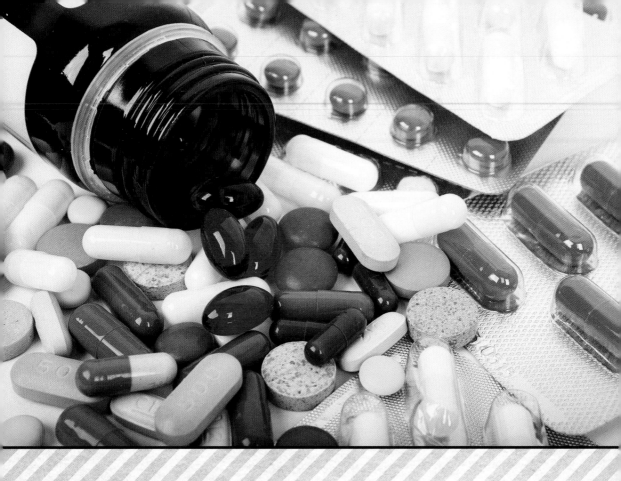

Critical World Issues

Abortion
Animal Rights
The Arms Trade
Capital Punishment
Consumerism
Drugs
Equal Opportunities
Euthanasia

Food Technology
Genetic Engineering
Genocide
Human Rights
Poverty
Racism
Refugees
Terrorism

CRITICAL WORLD ISSUES

Drugs

Jon Reese

MASON CREST
PHILADELPHIA

Mason Crest
450 Parkway Drive, Suite D
Broomall, PA 19008
www.masoncrest.com

Printed and bound in the United States of America.

CPSIA Compliance Information: Batch #CWI2016.
For further information, contact Mason Crest at 1-866-MCP-Book.

First printing
1 3 5 7 9 8 6 4 2

Library of Congress Cataloging-in-Publication Data

on file at the Library of Congress
ISBN: 978-1-4222-3651-2 (hc)
ISBN: 978-1-4222-8131-4 (ebook)

Critical World Issues series ISBN: 978-1-4222-3645-1

Table of Contents

1. Drug Use and Abuse 7
2. Recreational Drug Use Worldwide 23
3. The Global Drug Problem 33
4. Should Recreational Drugs Be Legalized? 43
5. Hooked on Medications...............................57
6. Alternative Medicines 69
7 Drugs and Sports 75
8. Effective Drug Treatments 85

Appendix: Drug Cartels..................................95
Organizations to Contact 98
Series Glossary...102
Further Reading...104
Internet Resources..106
Index...108
Photo Credits/About the Author.....................112

KEY ICONS TO LOOK FOR:

Words to Understand: These words with their easy-to-understand definitions will increase the reader's understanding of the text, while building vocabulary skills.

Sidebars: This boxed material within the main text allows readers to build knowledge, gain insights, explore possibilities, and broaden their perspectives by weaving together additional information to provide realistic and holistic perspectives.

Research Projects: Readers are pointed toward areas of further inquiry connected to each chapter. Suggestions are provided for projects that encourage deeper research and analysis.

Text-Dependent Questions: These questions send the reader back to the text for more careful attention to the evidence presented there.

Series Glossary of Key Terms: This back-of-the book glossary contains terminology used throughout this series. Words found here increase the reader's ability to read and comprehend higher-level books and articles in this field.

Drug Use and Abuse

Eighteen-year-old Suzie leads a life like that of many other teenagers. She studies and works hard in school, and hopes to go to college. She has many friends and a loving family, and plays soccer for her school team. Until recently, however, Suzie was also one of thousands of teenagers who take drugs—in her case, the drug ecstasy.

"The first drug I tried was cannabis, when I was fifteen," Suzie said. "A friend let me smoke a *joint*, but I didn't really like it very much. I kept smoking cannabis for a few months because a couple of my friends were really into it, and I just sort of went along with what they were doing. But I found that I was losing interest in things I enjoyed, such as sports, and sometimes I just couldn't be bothered to do my homework. I realized I had to stop taking the drug as I had tests coming up.

People take recreational drugs in a wide variety of situations such as this "rave." Dance music is closely associated with the taking of the drug ecstasy.

I'm really glad I did, as my two friends eventually dropped out of school completely.

"Last year, though, I started going clubbing. To begin with,

 Words to Understand in This Chapter

anesthetic—a drug that causes loss of feeling, and can be used to numb pain or make a patient unconscious during an operation.

depressed—feeling extremely sad and unhappy.

diabetics—people who suffer from the medical condition diabetes, where the body has trouble controlling levels of sugar in the blood and urine.

drug abuse—the taking of illegal drugs.

high—a feeling of exhilaration after taking drugs.

inhale—to breathe in.

insomnia—being unable to sleep.

insulin—a medicinal drug that diabetics need to take because they are unable to produce it naturally in their bodies.

joint—a cigarette that contains cannabis.

opiates—drugs made from the opium poppy, including opium, morphine, and heroin.

peer—someone of the same age or social group. Peer pressure is when people feel under pressure to behave "like the others."

pharmaceutical—to do with the preparing and manufacturing of medicines.

recreational drugs—drugs which people use for fun or leisure. Sometimes also referred to as "drugs of abuse."

relaxant—a drug that causes a person's mind or body to relax.

solvent—a substance that dissolves another. Solvents include gasoline and glue.

stimulant—a drug that speeds up physical processes.

synthetically—artificially, not naturally.

syringe—a device with a needle, used for injecting drugs into someone's body.

tranquilizers—drugs that make someone feel calm.

Drug users often frequent abandoned locations, such as this unused railroad station in Switzerland. Drug abuse is a problem in all countries and regions.

I never went anywhere near drugs, though there were loads of them around and people kept offering them to me. I just didn't want to go down that road again. On my last birthday, though, I got quite drunk and decided to take an ecstasy pill, as it was a special occasion. After that I took ecstasy most times I went to a club.

"It seemed great fun for a time, and I felt part of the 'in' crowd. But after a while I thought that I couldn't have fun unless I was taking drugs. I changed my mind after a couple of months. Ben, one of my new friends, suddenly stopped going clubbing. When I asked him why, he said he just couldn't han-

Drug Schedules

In the United States, the Controlled Substances Act of 1970 established five categories, or "schedules," of drugs. All pharmeceuticals—from ordinary prescription drugs to dangerous narcotics—are included on one of the following schedules:

- Schedule I controlled substances are considered to have no accepted medical use while also having a high potential for abuse. Examples include ecstasy, heroin, LSD, and marijuana.
- Substances on schedule II and III can be prescribed to treat medical conditions, but they are considered to have a relatively high potential for abuse or addiction. Schedule II includes both narcotics (such as morphine and codeine) and and stimulants (amphetamines and methamphetamine). Cocaine, which is sometimes used in certain medical procedures, is a schedule II drug.
- Schedule III includes products that contain multiple drugs, such as Tylenol with codeine, as well as anabolic steroids.
- Schedule IV and V controlled substances are drugs that have a medicinal purpose but have a relatively low potential for abuse or addiction. Schedule IV drugs include sleep aids like Xanax, anti-anxiety drugs like Valium, and muscle *relaxants* like Klonopin. Schedule V drugs include some types of cough syrup that contain several controlled substances.

The Controlled Substances Act established penalties that include heavy fines and imprisonment for the illegal sale or use of drugs.

dle it any more. He'd been taking ecstasy for the past three years, and he was sure it was making him *depressed*. He said that each week, a couple of days after taking a pill he felt so down he couldn't get out of bed. He'd been to see his doctor and they both agreed that he had to stop taking drugs and move on with his life.

"Although I never had any bad experiences like Ben's I decided it was time for me to stop taking drugs. I still go to clubs, and I enjoy it just as much as I ever did. You don't need to get *high* on drugs to have an amazing time. And I'm working really hard for my tests. I know that my future doesn't have to have anything to do with drugs, and I'm just grateful I never got into any real trouble when I used them."

What Are Drugs?

A *drug* is something that changes the way your body works. There are thousands of different kinds of drugs. Many are made from plants or from substances found in plants. Others are made *synthetically*, using chemicals in a laboratory.

Some drugs are used by people to change their mood and the way they feel about things. Some drugs, such as alcohol and nicotine, are legal in many countries. Other drugs—such as ecstasy, heroin, cocaine, or marijuana—are illegal. These mood-altering drugs are often known as *recreational drugs*.

Other drugs are medicinal. They can change the way you feel pain, or help your body to fight illness. Some medicinal drugs, such as certain painkillers or cold remedies, can be bought from a drugstore. Others, such as antibiotics used to fight infections, must be prescribed by a doctor.

Cannabis sativa is a plant grown all around the world and put to many uses, including the production of drugs. The plant thrives in many different climates.

Each year, new drugs are discovered or invented. Sometimes these are recreational drugs, but most of the time they are medicinal drugs produced by *pharmaceutical* companies to improve healthcare.

Recreational Drugs

There are many different kinds of recreational drugs. Worldwide, the most commonly used are amphetamines, cannabis, cocaine, ecstasy, heroin, and *opiates*. Some of these drugs, such as amphetamines and heroin, can also be used as medicines in certain cases.

Recreational drugs are sometimes described as "hard" or "soft." Hard drugs, such as heroin and cocaine, are considered to be more dangerous and addictive. Cannabis (also called pot, marijuana, and hash) is sometimes described as a soft drug, because it is less addictive than cocaine or heroin. But the terms "hard" and "soft" are not accurate scientific descriptions. The long-term dangers of a drug such as cannabis are difficult to measure.

Recreational drugs come in a range of forms. Cannabis is usually smoked, as is nicotine. Heroin can be smoked, *inhaled*, or injected into the bloodstream using a *syringe*. Cocaine

The flowers and leaves of the cannabis plant can be dried and processed into marijuana, a drug that is smoked or eaten to produce a mild high. Hashish is a similar, but more potent, drug produced from Cannabis.

comes as a powder, which can be inhaled through the nose. Other recreational drugs, such as ecstasy, are taken as pills.

The Effects of Recreational Drugs

Recreational drugs have very different effects, and the effects can vary from person to person. Drugs known as stimulants speed up how the mind and body work, while drugs called sedatives slow things down. Drugs called hallucinogens alter how a user senses things, and trigger hallucinations—seeing, hearing, or feeling things that are not really there.

Cannabis is the most commonly used drug in the United States and many other countries. It comes from the plant

Crystal methamphetamine, also known as "ice" or "speed," is a highly addictive stimulant that can cause serious health problems in users.

Cannabis sativa. Cannabis can take the form of a dried leaf ("grass") or a solid resin ("hash"). It is a mild sedative, and after smoking or ingesting it people often feel relaxed and happy. But users can also feel panicky or paranoid after taking the drug.

Cocaine, a white powder that acts as a strong stimulant, comes from the coca plant. Users often feel exhilarated and may have a sense of fearlessness. Other, less-pleasant effects can include a racing heart and *insomnia*.

Heating cocaine with baking soda and water creates a version of the drug called crack. This comes in small, rock-like pieces, which are usually smoked. The effects are similar to cocaine but tend to be more intense and short-term. Unlike many other recreational drugs, Cocaine does have some legitimate medical uses as an *anesthetic* in certain procedures.

Amphetamines and methamphetamine, also known as "speed," are stimulants. The effects are similar to cocaine, but tend to be less intense and to last longer. Amphetamines are a synthetic drug, as they are produced from chemicals in a laboratory. Amphetamines are often taken in pill form, while methamphetamine is usually in the form of a white powder.

Crystal meth is a form of methamphetamine that is particularly strong and highly addictive. It can be made in illicit drug labs, using a variety of toxic *solvents*. As a result, Meth labs can be extremely hazardous. Crystal meth can cause permanent brain damage and ruin a user's health. Despite this, many people in the United States and other countries use the drug because of the powerful "high" that it produces.

Ecstasy is a synthetic *stimulant* that is a mild hallucinogen. It can make users feel energetic and very friendly. They may also experience a dangerous increase in body temperature.

Heroin is a powerful sedative. Users feel an intense euphoria and sense of well-being, but first-time users are often violently sick. Heroin, opium, and morphine are all made from opium poppies and are known as opiates.

LSD (Lysergic acid diethylamide) is a hallucinogen. It produces hallucinations which can vary from fascinating visions and insights to terrible nightmares.

There are many other recreational drugs, and many substances that are used to achieve the same effect as these drugs.

 # Drugs and Addiction

Some drugs—such as cocaine, heroin, and crystal meth—are highly addictive. This means that after a certain amount of use, your body and/or brain begins to require the drug in order to function normally. The drug user starts to crave the drug when he or she stops using it. With some drugs, such as crack cocaine, it is possible to become addicted after trying the drug just a few times.

Alcohol and tobacco are legal in many countries, but it should not be forgotten that they too are addictive drugs. This is why many people who smoke or drink regularly experience great difficulty when they try to give up the habit. In fact, nicotine, the active ingredient in tobacco, is considered to be one of the most highly addictive drugs there is.

Illegal methamphetamine is often sold in powder form.

For example, fumes from gasoline or from solvents such as glue are sometimes inhaled to make the user hallucinate or experience a brief "high."

For most of the drugs listed above, the effects wear off after a few hours. With cannabis, there are no significant immediate after-effects besides an increased appetite. After taking a stronger drug like cocaine or ecstasy, though, the user is likely to feel tired and depressed. This feeling can sometimes last for a few days. Recreational drugs often have long-term effects, which will be explored in subsequent chapters.

Medicinal Drugs

The term *medicinal drugs* cover a huge range of products. Worldwide, the most widely used are painkillers and antibiotics, which sell in their hundreds of millions each year. In

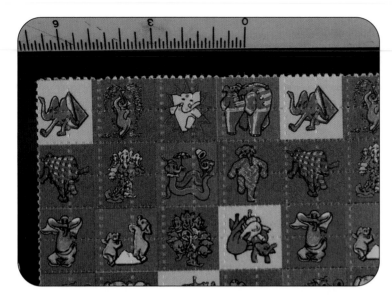

Lysergic acid diethylamide, better known as LSD, is a powerful drug that causes hallucinations. The drug is a clear liquid. It is often applied to small pieces of blotter paper, which can be held on the tongue to produce the effects.

2015, the best-selling brand-name drugs were Abilify, which is prescribed to treat depression; Humira, used to treat Crohn's disease and arthritis; Nexium, which can relieve gastrointestinal disorders; and Crestor, used to lower cholesterol in the blood. Each of them had sales of more than $1.3 billion that year.

With potential revenue like that, it's no wonder pharmaceuticals are a major industry. Millions of dollars are spent each year on developing new drugs and testing them so that they can be used safely. It can take years for new drugs to become available to consumers. Even with the strict regulatory process, there can still be concerns about how safe or addictive certain medicinal drugs really are.

Many medicinal drugs come in the form of pills or liquid medicines, which are swallowed. Some, such as the *insulin* needed by *diabetics*, are injected.

Why Do People Use Recreational Drugs?

Nearly all teenagers have heard of recreational drugs and their effects and know that many people around the world use them. It is hardly surprising, then, that they become interested in drugs and are curious to find out how drugs make you feel.

Some people imagine that taking drugs might be an enjoyable experience and a fun thing to do. Others are drawn to drugs because they are illegal and they feel that taking them is rebellious. They might also like the idea of doing something that is thought of as being dangerous. People also start taking drugs because of *peer* pressure. If their friends or family members are taking drugs, they feel they should follow the crowd and experiment themselves.

Some of the highest rates of *drug abuse* in the developed world occur in inner city areas where there is high unemployment and poor housing. People start using drugs because they are leading difficult lives and they feel it is a way to escape their everyday problems. However, drug abuse is not restricted to only certain areas.

Drug use tends to increase where there are particular problems, such as war or poor living conditions. In Iran, for example, it is estimated that 10 percent of the population regularly takes drugs. This is blamed on poverty, the low cost of drugs in the region, and a ban on the consumption of alcohol in the country.

In Syria, another Middle Eastern country, use of a powerful amphetamine called Captagon has drawn headlines in recent years. Since 2011 Syria has been devastated by a civil

Cocaine is a stimulant processed from the leaves of the coca plant. It is sold as a powder that can be inhaled or injected intravenously. Cocaine powder can also be processed into a crystal-like substance called crack, which causes an intense high when smoked.

war involving the government and various rebel groups, such as the Islamic State of Iraq and the Levant, which are also fighting each other. Soldiers on all sides of the conflict take Captagon to increase their energy so they can fight prolonged battles without needing to sleep. According to a United Nations report, Captagon produces a euphoric intensity that allows Syria's fighters to stay up for days, killing with a numb, reckless abandon. Many Syrian civilians are also experimenting with the drug, which sells for $5 to $20 a pill. Each year, illegal drug sales bring hundreds of millions of dollars into Syria's black-market economy, which can be used by militia groups to purchase weapons, pay fighters, and keep the conflict in Syria raging.

In a June 2015 report, the United Nations Office on Drugs and Crime (UNODC) estimated that 246 million people—

slightly over 5 percent of all people aged 15 to 64 years worldwide—used an illicit drug in 2013, the most recent year for which complete data is available. UNODC found that 27 million people are problem drug users, almost half of whom are people who inject drugs. From the data, the UNODC learned that men were three times more likely than women to use cannabis, cocaine, or amphetamines, while women were more likely to misuse prescription opioids and *tranquilizers*.

 Text-Dependent Questions

1. What effect do stimulants have on a person's body?
2. What are hallucinations?

 Research Project

Using the Internet or your school library, do some research to answer the question, "Should alcohol and tobacco be regulated like other recreational drugs?" Millions of people use alcohol and tobacco legally and responsibly today. However, they are both addictive and can cause health issues and social problems. For example, the long-term effects of smoking cigarettes kill over four million people worldwide each year, according to the World Health Organization. Present your conclusion in a two-page report, providing examples from your research that support your answer.

Recreational Drug Use Worldwide

People have been using recreational drugs for thousands of years. In 8000 BCE, people in Central America were using beans from the mescal plant as a stimulant. A form of this drug, mescalin, is still used by people today. There is also evidence from 5,000 years ago of cannabis use in central Asia and China.

Stone tablets from the ancient Sumerian civilization of Mesopotamia (modern-day Iraq) indicate that opium was used for pain relief and as a relaxant around 4000 BCE. The use of opium spread around the world. In modern times, smoking opium became a popular recreation in Europe during the seventeenth century. European traders introduced the habit to China, where addiction became so widespread that opium was banned by the government in the nineteenth century.

Marijuana buds are often rolled into a type of cigarette called a joint and smoked to create the "high" feeling.

Britain fought two wars with China over control of the lucrative opium market, from 1839-42 and 1856-60. These wars resulted in defeat for the Chinese, with the British Empire taking control of Hong Kong, and the opium trade continuing to flourish. By 1900, when opium was still legal in the United States and Europe, there were at least 200,000 Americans addicted to drugs which contained opium.

The leaves of the coca shrub, which is native to South America, have been used as a stimulant in some places in the world for over 4,000 years. Even today natives of places like Bolivia and Peru, where the shrubs grow well, brew tea from the leaves or chew them to gain a mild effect. Cocaine was first extracted from coca leaves in the 1860s. By the 1970s, cocaine had become popular among regular drug-takers.

Heroin was also developed during the nineteenth century. It was originally intended to help people who had become addicted to a drug called morphine. Doctors soon realized that the new drug was even more of a problem than the one it had replaced. Today, thanks to widespread availability in urban areas heroin addiction has become a major problem.

During the 1960s, the use of drugs like cannabis and LSD

 Words to Understand in This Chapter

trafficking—the transportation and trading of drugs between countries.
United Nations Drug Control Program (UNDCP)—a department of the United Nations which focuses on the world's drugs problems.

Coca leaves and cigarettes for sale in Potosi, Bolivia. The leaves provide a mild stimulant effect when chewed or brewed into tea, but can also be processed into the more powerful drug cocaine.

increased among young people in the United States and Europe. Then the explosion of dance music in the late 1980s led to a new craze with "dance drugs" such as ecstasy. The nature of taking drugs has changed continually over the centuries. It may well change even more in the future.

Global Drug Use

In the United States during the late 1970s, 14 percent of the population took recreational drugs. Today, the rate of drug use

A Yemeni man sells khat at the local market in Lahij, Yemen. Chewing khat, which is a stimulant that is moderately addictive, is a major social problem in Yemen.

in the US is about the same, but Americans are taking different kinds of drugs. More than 11 percent of Americans used marijuana during the previous year, according to the most recent data available from the *United Nations Drug Control Program (UNDCP)*. The study also found that about 4.3 percent of Americans took opioids, roughly 2 percent used cocaine, and another 2 percent used ecstasy or amphetamines. The United States, Canada, and Mexico combine consume more than 40 percent of the world's illicit cocaine.

South America, where most of the world's cocaine is produced, has largest problem with this drug. In Argentina, for example, about 3 percent of adults are regular users of cocaine. In South America as a whole, according to 2014 data, about 6 percent of all people used marijuana in the previous year, and about 2 percent had used either cocaine, amphetamines, or ecstasy.

The United Nations Drug Control Program (UNDCP) has noted an increase in the use of cocaine in Central America. It blames this increase on the continuing *trafficking* of drugs through this area. But overall drug use is relatively low compared to North and South America. The countries of Central

Chinese police escort Peter Gardner as he enters court in Guangzhou. In 2016 the Australian man faced a possible death sentence after being caught smuggling $25 million of methamphetamine.

A Liberian police officer watches as nearly 900 pounds (400 kg) of marijuana and other drugs are destroyed in Monrovia.

America have suffered in recent years due to drug cartel-related violence.

Recreational drug use in Africa is steadily increasing, with a sedative called methaqualone being among the most widely used drugs in the southern region. Overall, marijuana use in Africa is second only to North America, with about 7.5 percent of the population using the drug in the previous year, according to the UNDCP. (The Americas had the highest rate of marijuana use, at 8.1 percent.) Marijuana is particularly popular in West Africa, where more than 12 percent of all people have used it. Other recreational drugs are less common on the continent. Only 0.4 percent of adults used cocaine, and 0.2 percent have taken ecstasy. About 1 percent of Africans have taken amphetamines.

Addiction to opioids like heroin is relatively common in Asia. Officials in China have estimated that there are at least 1 million heroin addicts in the country. In places like Pakistan and Afghanistan, there are nearly four million people addicted to heroin and opium. Pakistan produces very little opium itself, but is flooded with the drug from neighboring Afghanistan, the world's largest producer.

A close-up of an opium poppy in Afghanistan. Money from the illicit sale of opium and heroin helps to fund Afghan warlords who are fighting for control of the country.

The second-largest producing region of the opium poppy is in southeast Asia—the "Golden Triangle" region where Laos, Myanmar, and Thailand meet. This has helped to fuel a major drug problem in southeast Asia. In recent years the governments of these countries have tried to curtail opiate production and use. They have not only failed to do this—by 2016, production of opiates from this region represented 30 percent of global cultivation—but restrictive laws have also led to the intro-

An injecting drug user arrives at a needle exchange bus in Geneva, Switzerland. Needle exchange programs allow drug users to obtain hypodermic needles and other necessary paraphernalia at little or no cost. The idea is to prevent infection with diseases like HIV and hepatitis, which can be spread when drug users share dirty needles.

duction of new drugs. Today, the most commonly used drug in southeast Asia is methamphetamine.

According to UNDCP data, nearly 11 percent of all Australians used marijuana during the previous year. About 1.5 percent used cocaine, while nearly 3 percent used ecstasy.

UNDCP found that drug use is higher in western and central Europe, with use rates that are similar to the United States. About 6 percent of western Europeans used marijuana during the previous year, according to the UNDCP data. About 1 percent of Europeans used amphetamines or esctasy, with a slightly higher rate of use in the countries of eastern and southeastern Europe. The European countries combined for more than 25 percent of the world's total cocaine consumption.

 Text-Dependent Questions

1. What is the native region of the coca shrub?
2. What share of the global cocaine market is consumed by North American countries?

 Research Project

Using the Internet or your school library, do some research to answer the question, "Does history show that taking recreational drugs is normal?" Some argue that if people were taking recreational drugs thousands of years ago, surely it is just a normal activity like eating and drinking. Others say that drugs were used in the past because of ignorance, but today we are better educated about the damage drugs do to our minds and bodies. Present your conclusion in a two-page report, providing examples from your research that support your answer.

The Global Drug Problem

In the United States, approximately 50,000 people die each year as a result of taking drugs. More than 20 percent of these deaths are a result of heroin overdoses. The 50,000 figure does not take into account the deaths of people who were infected by illness due to drugs, or whose drug use contributed to their deaths by exacerbating heart ailments or other physical problems.

The risks involved in taking drugs are not just about whether they kill you or harm your body. Drug abuse can also affect how a person's mind works—and the effects can be permanent.

When someone takes a drug, the immediate side effects can be very serious. In the case of ecstasy, the drug interferes with the body's ability to regulate temperature. If a user does not

A woman is arrested for possession of drugs at a national park in the United States. According to statistics from the Federal Bureau of Investigation, about 13 percent of all criminal arrests made in the US annually are drug-related.

drink enough fluids, this can result in overheating and sometimes death. Cannabis is known as a mild drug, but it too can be dangerous. When someone smokes it, the drug lowers their blood pressure. In some people this can lead to a stroke (bleeding in the brain) or heart failure.

With some drugs, *overdose* is the main risk. This is certainly the case with heroin. Sometimes the effects cause the user to forget how much they have taken, and they may take another dose. Because these drugs slow down the respiratory system, too much of the drug can cause a person to become unconscious or stop breathing.

In other cases, fatal overdoses occur because the drug is not pure. Unscrupulous drug dealers sometimes mix other substances into the drug, such as baking soda, caffeine, or mild anesthetics like benzocaine and lidocaine, so that they can

 Words to Understand in This Chapter

hepatitis—a disease causing inflammation of the liver.

HIV (Human Immunodeficiency Virus)—an infection which destroys the body's immune system and can lead to AIDS.

intravenous—into a vein, such as with an injection.

overdose—the taking of too many drugs, which can send the body into shock or even kill the user.

schizophrenia—a mental disorder in which sufferers are confused, sometimes hearing and seeing what is not there.

withdrawal symptoms—the unpleasant effects felt when somebody tries to give up a drug.

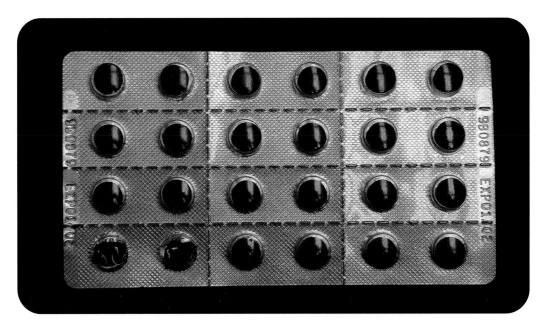

American laws make it very difficult for people to buy large quantities of over-the-counter medicines that contain pseudoephedrine, a key ingredient in the production of crystal meth. This has led to a major drop in the amount of methamphetamine made in the US— which created a new opportunity for drug cartels that can produce crystal meth in Mexico and smuggle it into the United States.

make more money from selling the same amount of the drug. These are known as cutting agents, because they are used to reduce, or cut, the amount of the actual drug that is sold to the consumer. However, if the drug is cut with a toxic substance, the results can be fatal. An overdose is also more likely to occur when drugs are cut because the user has no idea how pure or impure the drug he or she is taking actually is.

When someone injects drugs there is also the risk of contracting diseases such as *HIV* (Human Immunodeficiency Virus) and *hepatitis*. Recent statistics from the United Nations indicate that as of 2016, there are about 12.2 million *intra-*

An Afghan man walks into a drug treatment center in Jalalabad, Afghanistan. The artwork on the wall depicts a man who is bound up by opium poppies.

venous drug users worldwide. About 13.5 percent of this population, or 1.65 million people, are thought to be living with HIV. Four countries account for 63 percent of all people who inject drugs—China, Pakistan, Russia, and the United States. The HIV prevalence among intravenous drug users is highest in southwest Asia (29.3 percent) and eastern and southeastern Europe (22.8 percent).

Mental Dangers

According to the *British Journal of Psychiatry*, there is evidence that using cannabis can have a serious effect on mental health.

For some people, taking the drug can lead to psychosis (confusion and an inability to understand what is happening) and even to the serious mental disorder called schizophrenia.

Other drugs can also cause mental problems. Some LSD users report flashbacks to "trips" (the feelings you get when using the drug), sometimes many years after taking the drug. And many users of ecstasy report the "midweek blues," feelings of depression which may last for a few days after taking the drug. There are also reports that ecstasy can cause long-term or permanent depression and memory loss.

Mexican drug smugglers tried to use the hidden compartment on this truck to sneak bales of marijuana across the US border.

How do Drugs Affect Society?

People who take drugs are not the only victims of drug abuse. Heroin and cocaine addicts can spend tens of thousands of dollars every year on their habits. Most addicts cannot afford this, so they raise the money through crime. In Britain, the National Association for the Care and Resettlement of Offenders (NACRO) reported that people trying to get money for drugs committed one-third of all burglaries, street robberies, and thefts in 2015. The problem is a worldwide one. In Russia, the Public Health Ministry estimated that there were two million addicts in 2014, and that there were over 200,000 drug-related crimes in that same year. In South Africa in 2011, a study showed that more than 45 percent of crime suspects tested positive for at least one recreational drug shortly after they were arrested.

Drug abuse puts extra strain on health services and costs countries millions of dollars in education and policing. Many babies born to addict mothers have heart and lung defects. They are also likely to be addicted to the drugs their mother took when pregnant and to suffer *withdrawal symptoms* after they are born.

Over the past few years, people have grown more aware of the dangers of drinking and driving. However, the use of drugs while driving has increased. A US study of dangerous drivers found that over half of those who were not intoxicated with alcohol were under the influence of cocaine or marijuana.

A British report by the Automobile Association and the Association of Chief Police Officers found that in the previous 15 years, the number of people who had died in road accidents

American Drug Enforcement Agency (DEA) agents count cash seized in a drug raid.

as a result of taking drugs had risen from 3 percent to 18 percent of total road deaths. Police forces around the world are so worried about the problem that they are introducing detection kits to test whether drivers have been taking drugs.

Drugs and International Economics

Drug trafficking is a global illicit trade involving the cultivation, manufacture, distribution, and sale of substances that are subject to prohibition laws, such as recreational drugs. According to a UN study, the value of the trade in illegal drugs

In the US, laws have imposed mandatory prison sentences for people who are caught selling or buying illegal drugs. This has led to a huge increase in the prison population. Today, about 50 percent of the inmates in federal prisons and 20 percent of those in state prisons have been convicted of using or selling drugs.

around the world is $400 billion a year or more.

Some countries choose to move their economies away from reliance on the drugs trade. In 2000, the government of Myanmar announced plans to depopulate one of the world's biggest opium-growing areas in an attempt to halt heroin production. This would mean relocating 50,000 villagers in the remote Shan State, where little but opium poppies could be grown, to new agricultural areas near Thailand. In Pakistan, official figures show that in response to government efforts, opium production dropped from 700 tons in 1979 to around 10 tons in 1999.

Attempts to stop drug production are not always so successful. To help stop cheap cocaine coming into the country, the United States supported anti-drug operations in Colombia. As a result, production of cocaine decreased there for a time. In neighboring Peru, however, cocaine production increased due to greater demand for the drug because of the reduction of Colombian supplies.

 ## Text-Dependent Questions

1. What is a dangerous side effect of cannabis?
2. Why do fatal drug overdoses sometimes occur?

 ## Research Project

Using the Internet or your school library, do some research to answer the question, "Should marijuana be legal?" Those who are against legalization say that cannabis is a "gateway drug," with users more likely to move on to more dangerous drugs. They cite the example of Sweden, which has strict laws against all drugs (including cannabis) and consequently has one of the lowest rates of hard-drug use in Europe. Supporters of legalization will counter with the example of Holland, one of the countries that is most tolerant towards cannabis use, which has no higher rate of hard drug use than most other European countries. Present your conclusion in a two-page report, providing examples from your research that support your answer.

4

Should Recreational Drugs Be Legalized?

U ntil the late nineteenth century, there were no illegal drugs. Opium was widely available in the United States and Britain and was often used as an ingredient in "soothing" children's medicines. Cocaine was one of the original ingredients used in the popular soft drink Coca-Cola, although it was only present in tiny amounts.

In 1878, Great Britain passed the Opium Act, in an attempt to limit access to the drug and reduce the number of people taking it. Over the following years, more and more laws were passed in the United States, Britain, and other countries. Eventually, most drugs that are now considered recreational drugs were outlawed.

Many countries, including the United States, Britain, France, and the Netherlands, classify drugs according to how

Medical cannabis dispensary in San Francisco. In 1996, California became the first state to enact protections for medical cannabis patients when voters approved the Compassionate Use Act. Since then, twenty-three other states have passed laws legalizing marijuana for certain medical uses.

dangerous they are. Punishments for selling or using the more dangerous drugs are automatically more severe. Other countries, such as Sweden and Germany, do not automatically distinguish between different drugs, but leave it for courts to decide how serious they consider a particular offense.

In Britain, drugs such as heroin, cocaine, LSD, and ecstasy are known as Class A drugs. *Conviction* for possession can lead to a maximum seven-year prison sentence and a fine. Class B drugs include amphetamines (speed) and Class C drugs include tranquilizers and cannabis. With Class C drugs, the maximum sentence for possession is two years. Sentences for dealing drugs are always much more severe.

In the United States, all drugs, including medicinal drugs, are given one of five categories, or schedules. Schedule One represents drugs that have no accepted medical use, while Schedule Five includes over-the-counter medicines. In almost every state, a criminal conviction for a drug offense also brings with it the loss of the offender's voting rights.

 Words to Understand in This Chapter

convicted—found guilty of a crime.

legalize—change the law so that doing something, such as taking drugs, is no longer illegal.

prosecution—the arrest and trial of a crime suspect.

rehabilitation—recovery, restoring to a condition where somebody can play a full part in the world.

German activists collect signatures encouraging the government to legalize marijuana at Marienplatz square in Munich, 2015.

Why Are Some Drugs Illegal?

For decades, the US government has been waging a "war on drugs." Numerous laws have made it illegal to possess, manufacture, or sell dangerous, highly addictive drugs. Every year, Congress appropriates roughly $3 billion to the US Drug Enforcement Administration (DEA), a government agency that is responsible for preventing illegal drugs from being smuggled into the United States. Other federal agencies, such as the Border Patrol, Federal Bureau of Investigation (FBI), and US Coast Guard, also devote significant resources to the drug

Because drugs are illegal, every time someone takes them they are effectively a criminal. Should drugs be legalized, or at least decriminalized, so that drug users are no longer seen as criminals?

war. State and municipal governments spend billions each year on their own efforts to break up local drug rings and imprison drug dealers in their communities. In all, experts estimate that the United States spends more than $25 billion every year on anti-drug efforts.

However, these efforts have largely failed to prevent the flow of illegal drugs into the United States, or to reduce the number of Americans that use drugs. According to the annual Monitoring the Future survey conducted by the National

Institute on Drug Abuse, in 1991 just over 29 percent of high school seniors admitted to having used an illegal drug. Twenty-five years later, in 2016, that figure had risen to 40 percent. A 2012 study by the National Drug Intelligence Center found that illicit drug use costs the US economy more than $190 billion a year in lost worker productivity, increased health care expenses, and costs related to police activity and prison operations.

In the United Kingdom, two-thirds of the money that the government gives to tackling drug issues is spent on law enforcement, leaving only a small proportion for drug education and *rehabilitation* programs.

Should taking drugs be a matter of personal choice? Or do governments have a duty to use laws to stop people taking drugs? Some people argue that if drugs were legal, then more people would become users. They say this is reason enough for them to remain illegal. After all, it is a fact that drugs do kill and harm some users. Legalizing drugs would at least save the money that is spent on policing.

Others argue that some users take drugs because they like to break the law, and making drugs legal would make them less attractive. Some argue that taking drugs is just entertainment and, as it is statistically safer than pursuits such as driving and smoking, there is no reason for it to be illegal.

How Could Decriminalizing Drugs Help?

It has long been argued that crimes such as theft are such big problems in today's world because drugs are illegal. Francis

Wilkinson, a former senior police officer in Wales, said that heroin should be *legalized* in a bid to reduce street crime. He noted that because the drug is against the law, users have to find huge amounts of money to buy their drugs. Theft is usually the only way to do this.

Edward Ellison, the former head of the Anti-Drugs Squad in London, agreed. He said that he wanted to see all drugs legalized. This would remove the profit from organized criminals, who make so much money out of dealing in drugs. He also suggested that drugs should be manufactured by reputable companies. The companies could produce good- quality drugs, which could then be sold to users at reasonable prices.

Legalizing Marijuana

One drug in particular is discussed when people talk about making recreational drugs legal. Cannabis is used by millions of people around the world, and some countries have started to relax their laws in response to this.

Since the 1970s, people have been able to buy cannabis from coffee shops in Holland. The drug is still illegal, but the authorities do not *prosecute* anyone who has only a small amount of it. In Switzerland, cannabis weed can be sold in shops, but only if it is sold as products such as "tea" and "scent sachets"—but not as a drug. And in 2001, the Belgian government announced that it would move toward the decriminalizing of cannabis.

In 2000, a Police Foundation report in the UK suggested that cannabis should be downgraded from a Class B to a Class C drug, making arrest or imprisonment for using the drug very

In April 2016, Pennsylvania became the twenty-fourth US state to legalize medical marijuana. The drug can be prescribed as part of treatments for cancer, HIV/AIDS, Parkinson's disease, multiple sclerosis, epilepsy, glaucoma, and post-traumatic stress disorder (PTSD).

unlikely. It said that the harsh penalties for possessing and taking the drug were more harmful than the drug itself.

The government initially rejected the proposal. But in 2001, the Home Secretary went ahead and downgraded cannabis to a Class C drug. He said that the aim of the policy was to free the police to concentrate their time on dealing with harder drugs, such as heroin and cocaine. But he added that he had no intention of decriminalizing cannabis.

Cannabis plants grow inside a private greenhouse in the state of Washington. The medical marijuana law allows people who have received a prescription for therapeutic use to grow a certain number of plants for their own use.

The debate continues. Some think that governments which are lenient on soft drugs are encouraging drug use, and that this will inevitably lead to more users. Others say that the law against cannabis should be completely scrapped and that the drug should be as legal as tobacco and alcohol.

At the same time as announcing the reclassification of cannabis, the British Home Secretary stated that if clinical trials were successful, the law would allow the use of cannabis-based medicinal drugs. Sufferers of conditions such as multiple sclerosis and arthritis have said for years that cannabis is an effective treatment for the pain they endure. They have argued that they should be able to obtain the drug legally. In July 2001, Canada became the first country to legalize medicinal cannabis.

Marijuana is not legal in the United States according to federal laws. However, since 1996 a number of states have passed laws that allow people to use marijuana as part of their legitimate medical treatment for certain conditions.

In addition a few states have passed laws that permit people to possess small amounts of marijuana for recreational use. They include Alaska, Colorado, Oregon, and Washington, as well as the District of Columbia. It is still against the law to buy marijuana in these states, however.

Drug Education

Until the 1980s, drugs education was virtually non-existent. But as recreational drug use among young people increased, countries such as the United States and Britain realized that young people needed to be taught about drugs.

Initially, the message to young people was very simple. They were told to avoid drugs at all costs. Very little was said to them about the differences between drugs, or why people might want to take them. However, at the same time children started to learn about drugs from different sources. Children's television programs, for example, began to explain how drugs could affect children.

In the late 1980s and early 1990s, experts in drug abuse were employed for the first time to oversee drugs education in schools. Since this time, the approach to drugs education has changed a great deal. The general aim now is to inform young people about the dangers of drugs, but also about the reasons why people might want to take drugs. Young people learn exactly what effects drugs can have. Sometimes, children are even taught how to minimize the risks to themselves if they do choose to take recreational drugs.

Drugs education can include many different approaches. Education initiatives around the world have included inviting drug addicts to classrooms to talk to children about what it is really like to have a drug habit. This firsthand information can be a powerful deterrent for children who are thinking of trying drugs. Another approach is peer education, where young people with some knowledge about drugs talk to people of a similar age about the issues involved. Peer education can be particularly effective because young people are more likely to accept advice from those of a similar age, whose experiences of life are similar to their own.

The American Council for Drug Education, one of the nation's leading anti-drugs agencies, urges schools to introduce drugs education at a very early age. It has compiled lesson plans, activities, and worksheets which can be used by children from age four up to seventeen. Activities for older children include learning about peer pressure and how drugs can affect a user's health and appearance.

Drug Use in the Media

The first film to portray illegal drug use, *Reefer Madness*, was released in 1936. It depicted the smoking of cannabis as lead-

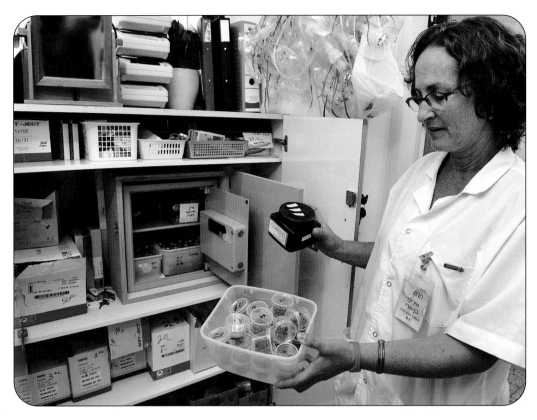

A nurse holds medical cannabis on July 17, 2011 in Rehevot, Israel. Although marijuana is illegal in Israel, it has been permitted for medical uses since the early 1990s.

ing inevitably to insanity. Since then, many films have been released about taking drugs. In 1994, *Pulp Fiction* received rave reviews but also much criticism, as some felt that it glamorized heroin use. Two years later, *Trainspotting* dealt in more depth with the issues, and the result was a film that vividly highlighted the bad side of heroin use.

Since then, films such as *Boogie Nights, Blow*, and *Traffic* have explored the reasons for, and the results of, drug abuse. The increasing visibility of drugs in films suggests how much a

Award-winning singer Whitney Houston died accidentally in 2012. The coroner determined that her use of cocaine contributed to her death.

part of modern society they have become. The hero of 1999's *American Beauty* smokes large amounts of cannabis, yet there were no negative comments about his drug use in reviews of the film.

Recent television shows have also featured drug use. The critically acclaimed cable television series *Breaking Bad* was about a science teacher who turns to making crystal methamphetamine to earn money for his family when he learns that he has cancer.

Films and television shows that give a balanced view of drugs and their dangers could be said to be setting a good example. But some of those who star in them fail to do so. In 2013 the young television star Corey Monteith died after taking a cocktail of illegal drugs. Hollywood star Robert Downey Jr. has spent time in prison and rehab due to his drug addiction.

Many famous and influential rock stars have also fallen afoul of drugs laws. In the past, stars including the Beatles's Paul McCartney and Mick Jagger of the Rolling Stones have been arrested for drugs offenses. The use of recreational drugs has always been seen as part of the "rock 'n' roll" lifestyle. But drug abuse has claimed the lives of stars—including Jimi Hendrix, Jim Morrison, and Janis Joplin.

Do people in the public eye have a responsibility to act as good role models? Even the former president of the United States, Bill Clinton, admitted to having taken marijuana when he was in college—although he claimed that he never inhaled!

 ## Text-Dependent Questions

1. What drugs are classified as schedule one in the United States?
2. How much does illicit drug use cost the US economy each year?

 ## Research Project

In the 1920s, the production and consumption of alcohol was banned in the United States. This was known as Prohibition. During Prohibition, crime rates soared, but fell when the ban was lifted and alcohol became legal again. Would crime rates fall in the same way if drugs were legalized today? Using the Internet or your school library, do some research to answer the question, "Would legalizing drugs reduce crime?"

Those who support legalization would say that Prohibition clearly shows that legalizing drugs would lead to a fall in crime rates. Those who want to maintain the current bans on illegal drugs will argue that criminals will use any excuse to make money. If drugs were legalized, they say, they would simply turn to different forms of crime.

Present your conclusion in a two-page report, providing examples from your research that support your answer.

5

Hooked on Medications

For thousands of years, people have been taking substances to relieve pain and cure disease. In the fifth century BCE, a Greek physician named Hippocrates used a bitter powder obtained from willow bark to ease aches and pains and reduce fever. The bark contained a chemical known as salicin—a similar substance to the active ingredient in modern aspirin.

Today, there are thousands of different pharmaceutical drugs available that are used to treat numerous afflictions. Medicinal drugs can be divided into three categories:

1. Those that treat the symptoms of illness
2. Those that are used in an attempt to cure illness; and
3. Those that prevent an illness from developing in the first place.

A machine packages pills for distribution in the retail market. Studies have shown that it costs between $4 billion and $11 billion to develop a new drug and bring it to market. The process also takes many years.

Over the past century, there has been a massive increase in the drugs available to treat the symptoms of illness. In the past, the only effective drugs you could use for pain relief were those made from opium, which were highly addictive. The many painkillers available today include ibuprofen and paracetamol. Drugs have also been developed to combat symptoms such as nausea and high blood pressure. These drugs do not actually cure the problems, but they can make a huge difference to someone's quality of life.

The discovery of penicillin in 1928 by Alexander Fleming was one of the major medical miracles of the twentieth century Penicillin was the first antibiotic. Before this, there were no medicines that could effectively treat bacterial infections and diseases such as tuberculosis, which killed thousands of people each year. Since the development of antibiotics, millions of lives have been saved.

Also during the twentieth century, vaccines were developed

 Words to Understand in This Chapter

AIDS (Acquired Immunodeficiency Syndrome)—the final, life-threatening stage of HIV infection.

anthrax—a potentially fatal bacterial infection.

antidepressant—a drug used to treat depression.

brand-name drugs—drugs which are made by a company and sold by a recognizable name.

side effects—unwanted effects from drugs, which occur at the same time as the main, desired effects.

Jenny takes the antidepressant drug Prozac. "Sometimes I can't cope with the kids and my job," she explains. "When things get tough, the doctor makes sure I get enough pills to help me for a few months. I'm not addicted, though. I can stop and start them when I like."

to prevent people from getting diseases. A vaccine usually consists of giving a patient a very small dose of a particular disease, so that their body develops an immunity to it. If the vaccinated person later comes into contact with the disease, he or she will not catch it. By the 1970s, the deadly disease smallpox had nearly disappeared due to a vaccination program. Other diseases, such as polio, have also been controlled by vaccines.

Today there are hundreds of vaccines available. These include drugs to prevent diseases such as measles, polio and

A doctor with the World Health Organization (WHO) administers a vaccine to a Haitian woman in Port-au-Prince.

flu. Scientists are even working on medicines to prevent people catching the common cold.

Side Effects

Everyone reacts slightly differently to the medicinal drugs they take. Some drugs work better for some people than for others, and some drugs are safer for some than others. Any drug that gets a license to go on the market has taken years to develop. This is why some drugs are so expensive when they are first released.

Although all medicinal drugs are tested vigorously, there are still questions over certain products. In Britain, scientists at the John Radcliffe Hospital in Oxford reported that over-the-counter painkillers such as aspirin and ibuprofen may be responsible for up to 2,000 deaths a year. They suggested that these drugs can cause dangerous internal bleeding in some patients. Aspirin is perfectly safe for most people who take it responsibly. But for a tiny minority who cannot tolerate the drug, even one tablet can kill.

Many medicinal drugs are relatively safe if taken in moderation, but taking too many can result in death. Overdose of another drug, acetaminophen, leads to more than 2,000 deaths worldwide each year.

Are Medicinal Drugs Addictive?

In the United States, a group of people launched a lawsuit against the makers of the *antidepressant* Seroxat. They claimed that when they stopped taking the drug they suffered disturbing withdrawal symptoms, including vertigo, agitation, and confusion. Some people said that these effects were so bad they could not stop taking the drug.

In 1988, all British doctors were issued guidelines about the addictive nature of tranquilizers, saying they should not be given to patients for more than four weeks at a time. Even so, more than a million adults in Britain were hooked on this medication by 2001, which was prescribed for them by their doctors. By 2016, it was estimated that more than 2 million Americans abuse tranquilizers each year. The symptoms of withdrawal from these drugs can be as painful and as lengthy as that experienced by addicts who try to stop taking heroin and other physically addictive drugs.

Today the most widely abused pharmaceuticals fall into three categories:

Opioids: These produce a sought-after euphoric effect due to their pain killing abilities for short-term or chronic pain.

Tranquilizers or depressants: these include barbiturates and benzodiazepines, some of the most abused drugs. They have a calming, relaxing effect, like a warm blanket on the brain.

Stimulants: These drugs increase brain activity, thereby increasing alertness and energy.

The Drug Abuse Warning Network (DAWN) says that Xanax is the most abused drug in the United States. Xanax is prescribed to treat anxiety. It calms a person by depressing his or her abnormal central nervous system. Some people abuse the drug, as well as other depressants like it, for their fast-acting sedating and relaxing effects.

Much like Xanax, the drugs Klonopin and Valium are often misused for their sedative effects. These "highs" can feel similar to the effects of alcohol, including feelings of drunkenness, talkativeness, and relaxation. All three of these drugs are considered potentially addictive, and there is a risk that taking too large a dose can cause a fatal overdose.

Oxycodone is a opioid that changes the way the brain and central nervous system respond to pain, creating a euphoric,

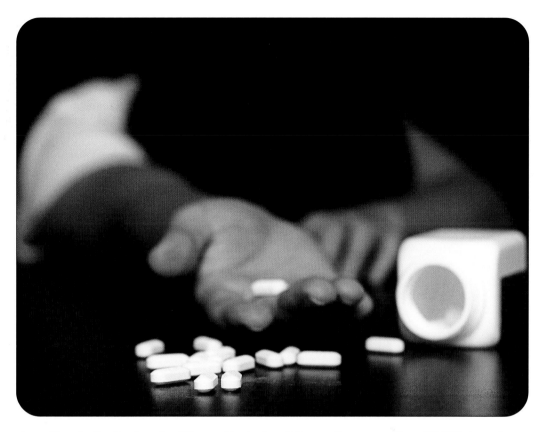

According to the Centers for Disease Control and Prevention, more than 25,000 Americans died from overdoses of prescription drugs in 2014, the most recent year for which data was available.

sedative effect. This drug is highly addictive. In 2006, the conservative radio talk show host Rush Limbaugh admitted to being addicted to Oxycodone and other painkillers after being arrested on drug charges.

Another commonly abused painkiller, Darvocet, was pulled off the market in the United States in 2010. In addition to being highly addictive, Darvocet was also was found to cause heart problems in some patients.

Changes for the Future

As diseases change and people around the world are looking to improve their quality of life, the companies that make medicinal drugs constantly have to find new drugs to meet the demand.

In the 1980s, a terrible new disease called Acquired Immuno-deficiency Syndrome, or *AIDS*, began to spread around the world. By 2016 there was still no cure, but pharmaceutical companies had successfully developed drugs which, when used in certain combinations, could lengthen the lives of people who were infected and even delay the onset of the disease.

Other illnesses, such as depression, have always been around but are becoming an increasing problem. The World Health Organization has predicted that by 2020, depression will be the second-largest killer in the world. Not surprisingly, drug companies have reacted to this news by researching and producing ever more effective medicines.

Drugs are also being developed for complaints that are not a direct threat to health. The release of the anti-impotence drug Viagra in 1998 was good business for its maker Pfizer. Viagra was initially meant to be a drug used for treating heart conditions, when doctors discovered its *side effects*. In the first two weeks after its release, over two million prescriptions were written for Viagra in the United States alone. In 2015, Viagra generated $1.7 billion in revenue for Pfizer.

An area of great concern for world health is the growing resistance of bacterial infection to antibiotics. Since the discovery of the first antibiotic drug, Penicillin, in 1928, these drugs have been widely used to treat illness in humans and animals. Antibiotics have saved millions of lives over the past decade. However, overprescription of antibiotics has led to some of them becoming ineffective, as diseases develop greater resistance. Some bacteria have changed through contact with antibiotics, and the original drugs cannot now kill them. Developing new antibiotics is seen as one of the most important challenges facing pharmaceutical companies.

The Cost of Producing New Drugs

Medicinal drugs are very expensive to develop. The companies that conduct the research on them get their money back by controlling the rights to produce the drug and by selling the drugs they produce. This has led to problems for poorer countries which have specific health problems.

In South Africa, there are well over four million people infected with HIV, the virus that can lead to AIDS. The government cannot afford the medicine to treat its citizens. But after much legal argument, pharmaceutical companies in the United States and Britain have agreed to let companies in South Africa copy their drugs and produce them at a much lower price.

In October 2001, a deadly disease called *anthrax* was deliberately spread in an act of terrorism in the United States. There has since been a fierce debate about whether governments should be able to buy cheap antibiotics to combat the disease from companies which do not hold the rights to produce them.

Sometimes, drugs that have been available for years see price increases in order to inflate a pharmaceutical company's profits. That occurred in 2015, when a drug company called

The headquarters of Novartis, one of the world's largest pharmaceutical companies, are located in Switzerland. Most drug companies are multinationals, meaning that they operate in many countries.

Turing Pharmaceuticals received a license to manufacture a drug called Daraprim, which is used in the treatment of malaria and HIV. This was not a new drug; it has been used since the 1950s. Because Turing held the only license to make the drug, it was able to increase the price by more than 5,000 percent, from $13.50 per pill up to $750 per pill. This led to outrage at the company and its CEO, Martin Shkreli.

Although Turing Pharmaceuticals's price hike was particularly high, other drug companies have also raised prices on established drugs in order to increase profits. A *Bloomberg News* report found that about twenty *brand-name prescription drugs* had quadrupled in price between December 2014 and February 2016, while another sixty medications have seen their prices more than double in the same time period. Pharmaceutical companies defend their actions by saying they have to raise prices in order to fund development of new medicines.

 # Text-Dependent Questions

1. What three categories do the most widely abused pharmaceuticals fall into?
2. How many people in South Africa are infected with HIV, the virus that causes AIDS?

 # Research Project

Using the Internet or your school library, do some research to answer the question, "Should medicinal drugs be tested on animals?" Those who support this view will argue that human life is so important that it is vital to continue testing to help provide safe medicines. Those who oppose it believe that more effort should be made to find alternatives to animal testing. In their view, animals have rights and feelings also. Present your conclusion in a two-page report, providing examples from your research that support your answer.

6

Alternative Medicines

Alternative medicines are those drugs and treatments that are not part of *conventional* Western medicine. The medicinal drugs prescribed by regular doctors are generally produced by large pharmaceutical companies. Alternative medicines generally rely on more naturally occurring substances, such as herbs.

There are dozens of different alternative treatments. Herbal medicine is one of the most popular. It involves using different plants to treat complaints from circulation and digestive problems to depression and stress. Usually the bark, flowers, roots, or leaves of plants are used to make a medicine that can be eaten or drunk, releasing chemicals in the plant which may help the patient.

Homeopathy is another very popular alternative health

Herbal remedies, containing plants, fungi, and animal extracts, are particularly popular in China and the developing world.

treatment. Experts in this field, called homeopaths, give patients highly-diluted doses of carefully chosen chemicals which in larger doses could be poisonous. No one really understands why this form of medicine works, but millions of people use it everyday and say that it is extremely effective. Because the doses used are so small, most scientists agree that it is safe.

Popular Treatments

The World Health Organization estimates that about 80 percent of the world's population uses herbal medicine more often than they use modern medicinal drugs. Most of the people who use alternative medicines live in poorer countries in the developing world. In these places, it is often much cheaper to obtain medicine from naturally occurring plants. Plus, such remedies are more common in traditional societies of Africa and Asia. But these alternative therapies are also becoming more popular in the Western world.

The number of alternative practitioners in the West is rising steadily. By 1999, the British Medical Association found that there were actually more alternative practitioners in the United Kingdom than there were licensed medical doctors. In

 Words to Understand in This Chapter

conventional—following accepted standards, or what is normally done.

homeopathy—the treatment of disease by minute doses of natural substances that in a healthy person would produce symptoms of disease.

Different types of vitamins and supplements on shelves in a pharmacy. According to studies, North America and Asia lead vitamin and supplement usage in the world.

the United States, a 2008 study found that approximately 38 percent of adults and approximately 12 percent of children were using some form of alternative medicine.

Are Alternative Medicines Safe and Effective?

Just because medicines are made from natural substances does not automatically mean they are safe to use. Herbal medicines can produce side effects just as conventional medicines can. Indeed, many modern drugs are produced from the same plants

Hypericum Perforatum, more commonly known as St. John's Wort, grows wild and is easily cultivated. It is a popular alternative treatment for mild depression.

that are used for alternative remedies.

Many experts question whether the standards are good enough for alternative medicines. They point out that it takes years of study to become a regular doctor, and years of research to test and produce a new pharmaceutical drug. But anyone can claim to be an alternative therapist, and remedies are easily available online for people to buy or sell.

One example of a popular alternative medicine is St. John's Wort, which has been used for years by traditional societies as a medicine. Some studies have indicated that St. John's Wort may be as effective as certain pharmaceutical drugs when used for the treatment of mild to moderate depression. St John's Wort has the additional advantages of having very few noticeable, short-term side effects and being much less expensive than conventional drugs. However, other studies have indicated that there is no evidence the plant actually works as a remedy. Nevertheless, consumers in the US, Canada, and Europe spent more than $6 billion on St. John's Wort supplements in 2015.

 ## Text-Dependent Questions

1. According to the World Health Organization, what percentage of the world's population uses herbal medicine more than modern drugs?
2. What condition do some people believe St. John's Wort is effective at treating?

 ## Research Project

Using the Internet or your school library, do some research on alternative medicines. Make a list of natural substances and the diseases or conditions that they are used to treat. Present your list to the class.

Drugs and Sports

7

In recent years, the financial rewards for top sports stars have soared. But as sport has become big business, there have been increasing numbers of cases where sports stars try to succeed by taking performance-enhancing drugs.

There are many drugs that athletes can use to improve performance, most of which are banned by the various sporting authorities. Some banned substances, such as steroids, can help athletes by increasing levels of a natural painkiller in their bodies. This allows them to train harder. Others, such as human gonadic choriotrophin, can boost muscle growth and help recovery from injury. In the long term, however, these drugs can be very harmful.

Of course, athletes sometimes take medicines just like everyone else, and they are allowed to take certain medicinal

Baseball player Barry Bonds finished his career with more home runs than any player in baseball history. However, his many accomplishments were tainted by the revelation that he had used performance-enhancing drugs to give himself an advantage over other players.

drugs. But even these can help improve performance—as can drugs such as caffeine, found in tea and coffee. This often leads to arguments about whether or not an athlete has deliberately cheated by taking drugs.

Who Are the Drug Cheats?

One of the first infamous drugs cheats was Canada's Ben Johnson. In the 100 metres at the 1988 Seoul Olympics, he won the gold medal and smashed the world record. Two days later, he was stripped of his medal after testing positive for *anabolic steroids*. After a second positive drugs test in 1993, Johnson was banned from competitive athletics for life.

Many other sports stars have fallen foul of drug use. In 1991, soccer star Diego Maradona of Argentina was banned from the game for 15 months after testing positive for cocaine. He was then sent home in disgrace from the 1994 World Cup, after having been caught taking a banned stimulant called ephedrine.

Another infamous cheater was Lance Armstrong, an American cyclist who won the world's most prestigious cycling race, the Tour de France, a record seven consecutive times from

 Words to Understand in This Chapter

anabolic steroids—drugs that increase body tissue, especially muscle.

dealers—people who deal in drugs, buying and selling them rather than just having them for personal use.

Lance Armstrong disappointed millions of fans and supporters when he revealed that prohibited drugs had helped him win many cycling races during his career.

1999 to 2005. Armstrong's story was amazing, as he had survived a life-threatening cancer before his run of success. This made him an inspirational hero to millions of people. However, although Armstrong had never tested positive for banned substances during his career, in 2012 an investigation determined that Armstrong had in fact used performance-enhancing drugs over the course of his career. Investigators found that he had used many tricks and schemes to hide the extent of his doping. Armstrong decided not to appeal the decision, and in 2013 admitted in a public interview that some of the charges were

American sprinter Tyson Gay celebrates after winning a 100-meter race in Greece, 2009. Gay holds the American record for that distance; his 9.69 second time is the second-fastest in history. However, in 2013 Gay was suspended from competition for a year after testing positive for a banned substance, and he was stripped of the silver medal that he won at the 2012 Olympics.

true. Consequently, Armstrong was stripped of his Tour victories, sued for millions of dollars, and his name was disgraced.

Two of the greatest baseball players of all time have also been linked to illegal steroids, which may have helped them to set records. Barry Bonds ended his career with more home runs than any other hitter in Major League Baseball history, 762. He also holds the record for most home runs in a single season, with 73. But he played out the last few years of his career under suspicion that he had been using performance-enhancing drugs. In 2007, Bonds was indicted for his involvement with the Bay Area Laboratory Co-operative (BALCO), an organization that provided illicit steroids to athletes. Bonds was convicted in 2011 on a charge of obstruction of justice, but the conviction was overturned in 2015. Nonetheless, despite have won an unprecedented seven Most Valuable Player (MVP) awards and being elected to fourteen All-Star Games during his career, Bonds has not yet been elected to the

Five time Grand Slam champion Maria Sharapova of Russia competes in a quarterfinal match at the Australian Open, January 2016. In March 2016, Sharapova was suspended by the International Tennis Federation because she had failed a test for performance-enhancing drugs. Sharapova had been a model and spokesperson for many companies, but she lost all of her lucrative contracts in the wake of her suspension.

New York Yankees star Alex Rodriguez was suspended for the entire 2014 season due to evidence that he had used performance-enhancing drugs. Only three players in major league history have hit more home runs that Rodriguez, who previously admitted using steroids from 2001 to 2003.

Baseball Hall of Fame, an indication of the stigma that drugs cast over the sport.

Similarly, Bonds's contemporary, Roger Clemens, put up some of the greatest single-season and career numbers for a baseball pitcher. Clemens finished his career with 354 career victories—the ninth-highest total all time, and the third-highest among all pitchers who played since 1920. He struck out 4,672 batters, the third-highest figure in MLB history. He won the Cy Young Award, given annually to the best pitcher in the league, a record seven times. Yet Clemens was also accused of taking performance-enhancing drugs at the end of his career. He was tried for perjury after denying that he had taken the drugs, but ultimately found not guilty in 2012. Nonetheless, many people believe that Clemens probably took performance-enhancing drugs, and like Bonds he has so far been excluded from the Hall of Fame.

The Accuracy of Drug Tests

In 1994, the British runner Diane Modahl was banned from competition for four years after urine tests showed a high level of testosterone in her body. Testosterone can enhance some athletes' performance, but Modahl insisted that she had not taken the drug. The next year, the ban was lifted after doubt was cast on the accuracy of the tests.

Many positive results for nandrolone, a banned performance-enhancing steroid, have been attributed to people taking dietary supplements or homeopathic medicines. In 2001, the Dutch footballer Edgar Davids used this excuse to explain the high levels of nandrolone found in his body—but he still received a five-month ban from the game. As performance-enhancing drugs become more sophisticated, it is increasingly difficult to identify the real cheats.

Occasionally, tests inaccurately determine that a person has been using drugs. In 2012, a Spanish lab that tested the blood of cyclists to make sure they were not using banned substances was suspended by the World Anti-Doping Agency for three months. The suspension occurred after the lab had determined that a particular cyclist had failed a blood test. A second test showed that the rider had not been doping, and research into procedures found that the lab had accidentally switched the rider's blood sample with another sample taken from a cheating rider. Recent studies indicate that between 5 and 10 percent of drug tests may result in "false positives."

Should Performance-Enhancing Drugs Be Legalized?

Most people believe that the use of performance-enhancing drugs is a violation of what athletics is all about. After all, at the highest level sports are meant to be an opportunity for the best, most talented athletes to compete against each other. Because the use of performance-enhancing drugs can give some competitors an advantage over others, most people support their being banned from sports.

But there is another school of thought that says that perhaps performance-enhancing drugs should be permitted at the highest levels of sport, so long as they are used with a doctor's supervision. Supporters of legalization believe that it would be easier to simply do away with the testing and enforcement regimes. It has often proven difficult to identify cheaters, so legalization would allow athletes to safely take drugs while also saving the time and expense used in treating for illicit drugs.

Supporters of legalization also say that it would be better for the athletes' health. Today, many athletes purchase steroids or other performance-enhancing drugs on the black market, from shady underground *dealers*. They often take the drugs without supervision by a doctor, which means the athlete may not fully understand what effect they will have on their long-term health. If performance-enhancing drugs were legalized, a doctor could work with athletes to make sure that they were taking substances in a way that was both safe and effective.

 ## Text-Dependent Questions

1. Why was Ben Johnson stripped of his Olympic gold medal?
2. What happened to Maria Sharapova after she failed a drug test in 2016?

 ## Research Project

Using the Internet or your school library, do some research to answer the question, "Do famous athletes have a duty to set a good example?"

Those who support this position would note that athletes are role models, and that getting involved with performance-enhancing drugs sets the worst possible example for their fans and followers. Others note that drugs can affect anyone—rich or poor, famous or unknown. If young people see their idols' lives being ruined or ended by drugs, they will realize that it could easily happen to them. Nothing could be more effective in making young people choose not to take drugs.

Present your conclusion in a two-page report, providing examples from your research that support your answer.

Effective Drug Treatments

M any users do stop taking recreational drugs, sometimes with the help of special treatment. But until the 1970s, the only way for most people to end their drug abuse was simply to stop taking the drugs. This was often very unpleasant—especially if the drug was addictive. Today, there are alternatives for those looking to kick their habit.

If users want to stop taking heroin, a doctor may offer them a synthetic medicine called *methadone*. This drug produces feelings similar to those produced by heroin, but it is not as strong or addictive. Addicts sometimes find it is a step towards giving up their dependency on heroin. Unfortunately, methadone also has side effects, which are similar to those of

Exercise classes are an increasingly popular pastime, encouraging the body to produce its own natural chemicals.

the drug it replaces. If too much methadone is taken, it can result in a fatal overdose.

Scientists are working on other means to help drug addicts. They are in the process of developing a vaccine which they believe could help make cocaine users immune to the effects of the drug, making it pointless for them to take it. The drug, known as TA-CD, has undergone clinical trials. If further tests are successful, it could be available to addicts within a few years.

Young people can get enjoyment from life in a variety of ways. For some, studying is the most important thing in their lives, as they wish to get good test results and rewarding jobs in the future. Others play sport, which keeps them fit and can also be extremely rewarding. Activities like these can give a sense of achievement which is much more real and long-lasting than the artificial "highs" that any drug could ever give. Relationships with friends and family also give individuals pleasure and are another way in which people can lead meaningful lives. Drugs hold a strong appeal for some people. But they are never the only way to get something out of life, and they frequently lead to misery rather than enjoyment.

 Words to Understand in This Chapter

endorphins—hormones in the brain that reduce the sensation of pain and affect emotions.

methadone—a synthetic drug that is used as a substitute drug in the treatment of morphine and heroin addiction.

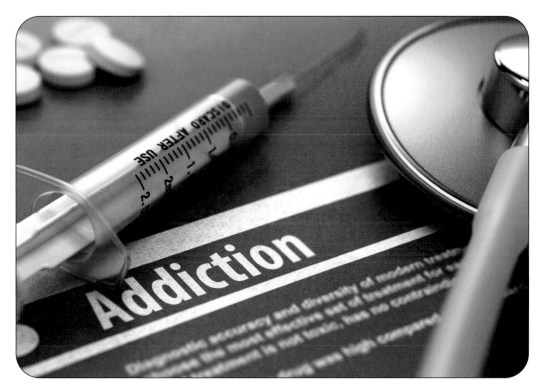

The goals of drug treatment include ending the abuse of drugs, while also helping the user to once again become a productive member of a family or community.

Can rehabilitation work?

People who want to stop taking drugs often find it helps them to talk to a professional counselor. They can talk about why they took drugs in the first place, how to cope with withdrawal symptoms, and life after drugs. Sometimes, drug users are also placed in rehabilitation programs. These can provide a safe place for a few days or weeks, where there are no illegal drugs and there is plenty of counselling available. Courts have the option of sending convicted drug offenders into rehabilitation programs.

Rehabilitation is considered an extremely useful tool for breaking the cycle of drug dependence. In 2016, the Office of National Drug Control Policy spent about 43 percent of its annual budget—over $13.4 billion—on drug treatment programs.

According to the annual National Survey on Drug Use and Health, conducted by the Substance Abuse and Mental Health Services Administration (SAMHSA), there is a large "treatment gap" in the United States. In 2013, the most recent year for which data is available, an estimated 22.7 million Americans (8.6 percent of the total population) needed treatment for a problem related to drugs or alcohol. However, only about 2.5 million people (0.9 percent) received treatment at a specialty facility.

A Worldwide Problem

In many countries around the world, the vast majority of the population does not take recreational drugs. Even in Britain

 Feeling Fit

In the United States and Europe, over 10 million people are members of fitness centers. Those who attend fitness classes or go to gyms get a natural buzz from controlling their own fitness, losing weight and improving their health. Their bodies also produce chemicals called *endorphins* while they are exercising. This is a natural drug which helps them feel relaxed and happy for many hours afterward.

Popular actor Robert Downey Jr. has battled drug addition for many years.

and the United States, two of the world's largest consumers of drugs, most people have never taken them.

However, drug use is definitely a problem. In many countries, particularly in the Far East and Africa, drug abuse is on the increase. With drug abuse come the problems associated with it, namely crime and poor health. For those in any country who suffer from addiction, or for those who are the victims of drug-related crime, drugs continue to be an enormous burden.

What the Future Holds

No one knows exactly what will happen in the future. Will drugs that are currently illegal become legal? Will scientists find cures for the many killer diseases in the world? The only thing that is certain is that there will be changes in how we use and view drugs in our lives.

Two hundred years ago there were no illegal drugs. Could it be that in another two centuries the same will be true? Cannabis laws certainly seem to be changing. Will those who wish to use cannabis be able to buy the drug in shops or bars soon as easily as smokers and drinkers can buy their chosen drugs now?

What about hard drugs? Legalizing drugs such as heroin and cocaine might reduce crime, but should society ever be seen to be condoning or encouraging their use? And what new recreational drugs might be invented or discovered in the future? The past three decades years have seen the emergence

 ## Brave New World

In his 1932 novel *Brave New World*, author Aldous Huxley describes a world in the future where everyone takes a drug called Soma, making them feel content. In a way, his prediction has come true. Every year, tens of millions of people use antidepressants to improve their mood. The World Health Organization predicts that this figure will rise by millions over the next few years.

of "designer drugs," such as ecstasy and Mephedrone. In the next few years, an entirely new recreational drug might become popular. How might such a drug be used, and what part might it play in a future society?

Will Drugs Change the World of Medicine?

Scientists are constantly working to produce new medicinal drugs. Some are trying to develop drugs that can slow down the aging process. Others are looking for drugs to improve intelligence. And the quest to find medicines that can cure killer diseases such as cancer, HIV, and heart disease is the focus of huge amounts of work. Scientists are also finding new uses for medicinal drugs which have been around for years. Aspirin has been found to help fight heart disease—and even thalidomide, responsible for so many terribly deformed babies, is being hailed as a weapon against certain cancers.

Genetic engineering, with which scientists can alter the structure of living organisms, is certain to be an important factor in the development of new drugs. Scientists may become able to use genetic engineering to design their own drugs, which work in particular ways. There will then be virtually no limits to what drugs might be available to treat disease in the future.

The race has already begun to find drugs which can replace the antibiotics which are fast becoming ineffective in fighting disease. This, and other research into medicinal drugs, may become vital to our very existence.

Text-Dependent Questions

1. What are some ways that young people can get enjoyment from life without turning to drugs?
2. What percentage of Americans received treatment for drug or alcohol abuse in 2013?
3. How might genetic engineering affect drugs in the future?

 Research Project

Using the Internet or your school library, do some research to answer the question "Should the use of recreational drugs be a personal choice?"

Some people believe that everyone should have the right to do whatever they like, and this includes taking illegal drugs if they want to. What right does any government have to tell you what to do with your body, they contend?

Those who disagree with this perspective note that drugs are not only dangerous for those who take them, but can lead to crime and other social problems that affect others. The authorities should take a tough line against drugs and their users, and encourage people to lead drug-free lives, they believe.

Present your conclusion in a two-page report, providing examples from your research that support your answer.

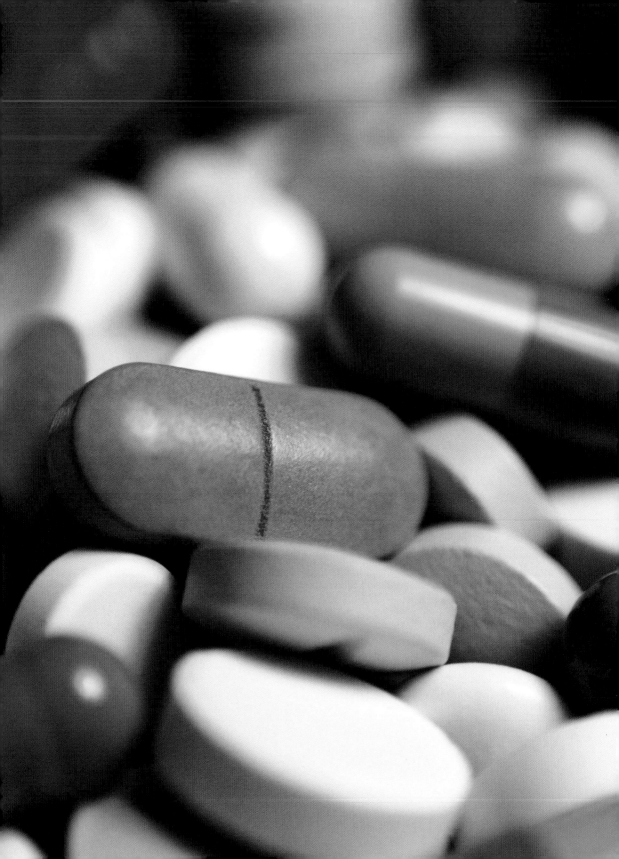

Appendix

Drug Cartels

T he failure of the American drug war is due in large part to the success of well-organized and well-financed drug selling operations, often referred to in the media as "drug cartels."

A cartel is an association of businesses that agree to work together in order to set the price for a commodity or service that they control. One well-known example of a legitimate cartel is OPEC, an international association of countries that possess significant oil reserves. OPEC affects the global price of oil by regulating the amount of oil that its members produce each year. The term *drug cartels* originated in the 1980s, when some of the major cocaine dealers in Colombia agreed to work together on production and distribution of that drug. Today, the term is popularly used to refer to any criminal organization that makes its money primarily from manufacturing, smuggling and distributing illegal drugs. In official reports the DEA, FBI, and other government agencies often refer to drug cartels as "drug trafficking organizations," or DTOs.

Today the Colombian drug cartels are no longer as power-ful, largely because of the anti-drug policies known as Plan Colombia that the country's government implemented in the early 2000s. Instead, drug cartels from Mexico have come to dominate the global trade in illegal drugs over the past two decades. The Mexican cartels, such as the notorious Sinaloa Cartel, operate like international corporations—they make partnerships with street gangs and crime organizations in the United States and other countries in order to distribute drugs. As a result, the Sinaloa Cartel earns an estimated $20 billion a year in profits from its drug smuggling and selling operations. The Sinaloa Cartel's leader, Joaquín "El Chapo" Guzmán, was arrested in Mexico in 2014, escaped from prison the next year, and was recaptured in January 2016.

Cartels from Central America, the Caribbean, Central Asia, Africa, China, and Russia also work in much the same way, controlling their own shares of illegal drug markets in the United States, Europe, and other places.

The enormous amounts of money that the cartels can earn makes them willing to take risks and spend money to make sure their drug shipments can get into the United States. Since the 1970s, the U.S. government has declared a "war on drugs," with many laws passed to stop the flow of drugs into the coun-try and bring down drug dealers.

Another focus of the drug war has been to prevent drugs from coming into the United States. Federal agencies like the U.S. Border Patrol, U.S. Coast Guard, DEA, and FBI, among others, have been charged with preventing drug smuggling into the United States. Every year the leaders of these agencies announce numerous seizures of large drug shipments. However, as with the arrests of drug dealers, experts today agree that these busts hardly affect the operation, or the profits, of drug cartels.

For example, when authorities intercept a large shipment of cocaine, this should cause the street price of cocaine to rise. This is because of the economic law known as "supply and demand"—if the bust meant less of the drug was available, it could be sold for a higher price. What has actually happened, however, is that despite hundreds of highly publicized seizures, the street price of cocaine in the United States is less than half of what it was 20 years ago. In 1992, according to DEA data, a gram of cocaine cost about $245; in 2012 that gram of coke cost about $110, with the price of a gram as low as $75 in some places. The prices of other drugs, such as marijuana and methamphetamine, are also lower now than they were two decades ago. This fact is a testament to the success that drug cartels have had getting their illegal products to users in the United States. For every shipment that is captured, many more pass over the border undetected.

Mexico has become a key nexus of the illegal drug trade because of its location between the United States and the major drug-producing countries of Central and South America. The FBI reports that more than 90 percent of the illegal drugs smuggled into the United States today come across the border from Mexico.Ω

Organizations
to Contact

Alcoholics Anonymous

Grand Central Station

PO Box 459

New York, NY 10163

(212) 870-3400

Website: www.aa.org

Centers for Disease Control and Prevention

Office of Communication

Building 16, D-42

1600 Clifton Road, N.E.

Atlanta, GA 30333

(800) 311-3435

Website: www.cdc.gov

Drug Enforcement Administration

2401 Jefferson Davis Highway

Alexandria, VA 22301

(202) 307-1000

Website: www.usdoj.gov/dea

Mothers Against Drunk Driving

511 E. John Carpenter Freeway, Suite 700

Irving, TX 75062

(800) GET-MADD

Website: www.madd.org

Narcotics Anonymous

PO Box 9999

Van Nuys, CA 91409

(818) 773-9999

Website: www.na.org

National Drug Intelligence Center

319 Washington Street, 5th Floor

Johnstown, PA 15901-1622

(814) 532-4601

Website: www.usdoj.gov/ndic

National Institute on Alcohol Abuse and Alcoholism

5635 Fishers Lane, MSC 9304

Bethesda, Maryland 20892-9304

(800) 662-HELP

Website: www.niaaa.nih.gov

National Institute on Drug Abuse

6001 Executive Boulevard, Room 5213

Rockville, MD 20852

(301) 443-1124

Website: www.nida.nih.gov

National Organization for Reform of Marijuana Laws

1600 K Street NW

Suite 501

Washington, DC 20006-2832

(202) 483-5500

Website: www.norml.org

Partnership for a Drug Free America

405 Lexington Avenue, Suite 1601

New York, NY 10174

(212) 922-1560

Website: www.drugfreeamerica.org

Substance Abuse and Mental Health Services Administration

1 Choke Cherry Road

Room 8-1054

Rockville, MD 20857

(240) 276-2000

Website: www.samhsa.gov

White House Office of National Drug Control Policy

Drug Policy Information Clearinghouse

PO Box 6000

Rockville, MD 20849-6000

(800) 666-3332

Website: www.whitehousedrugpolicy.gov

Series Glossary

apartheid—literally meaning "apartness," the political policies of the South African government from 1948 until the early 1990s designed to keep peoples segregated based on their color.

BCE and CE—alternatives to the traditional Western designation of calendar eras, which used the birth of Jesus as a dividing line. BCE stands for "Before the Common Era," and is equivalent to BC ("Before Christ"). Dates labeled CE, or "Common Era," are equivalent to *Anno Domini* (AD, or "the Year of Our Lord").

colony—a country or region ruled by another country.

democracy—a country in which the people can vote to choose those who govern them.

detention center—a place where people claiming asylum and refugee status are held while their case is investigated.

ethnic cleansing—an attempt to rid a country or region of a particular ethnic group. The term was first used to describe the attempt by Serb nationalists to rid Bosnia of Muslims.

house arrest—to be detained in your own home, rather than in prison, under the constant watch of police or other government forces, such as the army.

reformist—a person who wants to improve a country or an institution, such as the police force, by ridding it of abuses or faults.

republic—a country without a king or queen, such as the US.

United Nations—an international organization set up after the end of World War II to promote peace and co-operation throughout the world. Its predecessor was the League of Nations.

UN Security Council—the permanent committee of the United Nations that oversees its peacekeeping operations around the world.

World Bank—an international financial organization, connected to the United Nations. It is the largest source of financial aid to developing countries.

World War I—A war fought in Europe from 1914 to 1918, in which an alliance of nations that included Great Britain, France, Russia, Italy, and the United States defeated the alliance of Germany, Austria-Hungary, the Ottoman Empire, and Bulgaria.

World War II—A war fought in Europe, Africa, and Asia from 1939 to 1945, in which the Allied Powers (the United States, Great Britain, France, the Soviet Union, and China) worked together to defeat the Axis Powers (Germany, Italy, and Japan).

Further Reading

Campos, Isaac. *Home Grown: Marijuana and the Origins of Mexico's War on Drugs*. Chapel Hill: University of North Carolina Press, 2012.

Hari, Johann. *Chasing the Scream: The First and Last Days of the War on Drugs*. New York: Bloomsbury, 2015.

Kuhn, Cynthia, et al. *Buzzed: The Straight Facts about the Most Used and Abused Drugs from Alcohol to Ecstasy*. New York: W.W. Norton, 2008.

Levinthal, Charles F. *Drugs, Behavior, and Modern Society*, 8th ed. New York: Pearson, 2013.

Longmire, Sylvia. *Cartel: The Coming Invasion of Mexico's Drug Wars*. Palgrave Macmillan, 2011.

Quinones, Sam. *Dreamland: The True Tale of America's Opiate Epidemic*. New York: Bloomsbury, 2016.

Internet Resources

www.justice.gov/dea/index.shtml

The Drug Enforcement Administration is the government agency charged with investigating the illegal narcotics trade in the United States. The DEA, which is part of the US Department of Justice, also helps local police departments track and arrest drug dealers.

www.monitoringthefuture.org

The University of Michigan publishes an annual report on drug use by young people, *Monitoring the Future*, which can be accessed at this site.

www.whitehouse.gov/ondcp

The White House Office of National Drug Control Policy develops a national strategy to combat illegal drug use and serves as a liaison linking the different federal drug investigation and research agencies.

www.fas.org/sgp/crs/row/RL34215.pdf

This site contains a report prepared for the US Congress by an analyst in Latin American affairs. The report "provides an overview of: Mexican cartels and their operations, including the nature of cartel ties to gangs; Mexican cartel drug production in the United States; and the presence of Mexican cartel cells in the United States."

www.pbs.org/wgbh/pages/frontline/shows/drugs
Companion website to the PBS Frontline documentary *Thirty Years of America's Drug War.*

www.camy.org
The Center on Alcohol Marketing and Youth (CAMY) at Johns Hopkins University employs a public health approach to prevent and reduce alcohol-related problems among young people.

Index

addiction, drug, 16, 61–63, 85–86
    and rehabilitation, 44, 47,
        85–88
    See also drug abuse
Afghanistan, 29, **36**
Africa, 28–29, 65, 70, 89
AIDS (Acquired Immunodeficiency
    Syndrome), 58, 64, 65
alcohol, 11, 16, 88
alternative medicines, 69–73
    See also medicinal drugs
American Council for Drug
    Education, 52
amphetamines, 10, 12, 15, 19–20,
    21, 44
    and number of users, 26, 27,
        29, 31
antibiotics, 11, 17, 58, 64–65, 92
    See also medicinal drugs
antidepressants, 58, **59**, 61, 64, 90
    and St. John's Wort, 72–73
Armstrong, Lance, 76–78
Asia, 23–24, 29–31, 36, 70, 89

Bay Area Laboratory Co-operative
    (BALCO), 79
    See also performance-enhancing
        drugs
Bonds, Barry, **75**, 78–80
Brave New World (Huxley), 90
Breaking Bad (TV show), 54

Canada, 26, 51
Cannabis sativa, 12, 14–15
    See also marijuana (cannabis)
Captagon, 19–20
cartels, drug, 28, **35**, 95–97
    See also crime
Central America, 23, 27–28
China, 23–24, 29, 36
classes, drug, 43–44, 48–49, 50–51
    See also schedules, drug
Clemens, Roger, 80–81
cocaine, 10, 12–14, 15, 16, **20**, 21,
    25, 40–41, 44, **54**, 86, 95
    in history, 24, 43
    and number of users, 26–27,
        29, 31
    price of, 97
Colombia, 40–41, 95–96
Controlled Substances Act of 1970,
    10
crack cocaine, 15, 16, **20**
crime, **33**, 38–41, 48, 89
    and drug cartels, 28, **35**, 95–97
    and drug trafficking, 24, 27, **37**,
        39–41
    and prison sentences, **40**, 44
    See also drug abuse
crystal methamphetamine, **14**, 15,
    16, **35**

Darvocet, 63

Numbers in ***bold italics*** refer to captions.

Davids, Edgar, 81
"designer drugs," 92
Downey, Robert, Jr., 54, 89
drug abuse, 47
    and addiction, 16, 44, 47,
      61–63, 85–88
    and crime, 28, *33*, *35*, 38–39,
      40, 44, 48, 89, 95–97
    and driving, 38–39
    and number of people using
      drugs, 19, 20–21, 25–27,
      28–31, 46–47, 88–89
    reasons for, 19–21
    and rehabilitation, 44, 47,
      85–88
    rising rates of, 89, 90
    and withdrawal symptoms, 34,
      38, 61–62
    See also medicinal drugs; per-
      formance-enhancing drugs;
      recreational drugs
Drug Abuse Warning Network
    (DAWN), 62
Drug Enforcement Agency (DEA),
    39, 45
"drugs of abuse." *See* recreational
    drugs

ecstasy, 7–9, 10, 11, 12, 14, 16, 25,
    44, 92
    and number of users, 26, 27,
      29, 31
    side effects of, 33–34, 37
education, drug, 51–52
Ellison, Edward, 48
endorphins, 86, 88
Europe, 31, 36

Fleming, Alexander, 58

Great Britain, 24, 38–39, 43, 44,
    47–49, 50–51, 61
alternative medicine practitioners

in, 70
Guzmán, Joaquín ("El Chapo"), 96

hallucinogens, 14, 16
"hard" drugs. *See* recreational drugs
hash. *See* marijuana (cannabis)
hepatitis, 34, 35–36
herbal medicines, 69, 70, 71–73
heroin, 8, 10, 12–13, 16, 40, 44, 48,
    85–86
    in history, 24
    and number of users, 29
    overdoses, 33, 34
Hippocrates, 57
HIV (Human Immunodeficiency
    Virus), *30*, 34, 35–36, 65, 66
homeopathy, 69–70
    See also alternative medicines
human gonadic choriotrophin, 75
    See also performance-enhancing
      drugs

Johnson, Ben, 76

khat, *26*
Klonopin, 10, 62

laws, anti-drug, 43–44, 45
    See also crime
Limbaugh, Rush, 63
LSD (Lysergic acid diethylamide),
    10, 16, *18*, 24–25, 37, 44

Maradona, Diego, 76
marijuana (cannabis), 10, 12–13,
    14–15, 17, 21, 44, 97
    in history, 23, 24–25
    legalization of, *43, 45*, 48–51,
      90
    in the media, 52–53
    medical use of, *43, 49*, 50–51,
      53
    and mental health, 36–37

and number of users, 26, 27, 28–29, 31
side effects of, 34
See also medicinal drugs; recreational drugs
media, 52–55
medicinal drugs, 8, 11, 17–18, 66–67, 69, 92
   addiction to, 61–63
   antibiotics, 11, 17, 58, 64–65, 92
   cost of development of, 12, 18, **57**, 60, 64–67
   and drug schedules, 10, 44
   and side effects, 58, 60–61, 64
   types of, 57–60
   See also alternative medicines; drug abuse; performance-enhancing drugs; recreational drugs
methadone, 85–86
methamphetamine, 10, 15, *17*, 31, *35*, 97
Mexico, 26, *35, 37*, 96
Modahl, Diane, 81
Monteith, Corey, 54
morphine, 8, 10, 16, 24
Myanmar, 30, 40

National Association for the Care and Resettlement of Offenders (NACRO), 38
needle exchange programs, **30**
nicotine, 11, 13, 16

opiates, 8, 12, 16, 21, 30–31
opioids, 26, 29–31, 62–63
opium, 8, 16, 23–24, 29, 40, 43, 58
Opium Act, 43
overdose deaths, 33, 34–35, 55, 61, **63**
Oxycodone, 62–63

Pakistan, 29, 36, 40
penicillin, 58, 64–65
performance-enhancing drugs, 75–82
legalization of, 82–83
pharmaceutical companies, 12, 64–67, 69
   See also medicinal drugs
prison sentences, **40**, 44
   See also crime

recreational drugs, 8, 11–17, 39–40
   cost of, 97
   and drug schedules, 10, 44
   future of, 90–91
   global use of, 25–31
   and history of use, 23–25
   and laws, 43–44, 90
   legalization of, *43, 45*, 47–51, 90
   in the media, 52–55
   and mental health, 36–37
   and reasons for use of, 19–21
   side effects of, 15–16, 17, 33–37
   treatments for, 85–86
   types of, 12–14
   See also drug abuse; medicinal drugs; performance-enhancing drugs
Reefer Madness (movie), 52–53
rehabilitation, drug addiction, 44, 47, 85–88
   See also drug abuse
research projects, 21, 31, 41, 55, 67, 73, 83, 93

salicin, 57
schedules, drug, 10, 44
   See also classes, drug
schizophrenia, 34, 37
sedatives, 14, 15, 16
Shkreli, Martin, 66

Sinaloa Cartel, 96
    See also cartels, drug
"soft" drugs. *See* recreational drugs
South America, 24, 26–27
speed. *See* amphetamines
sports
    and accuracy of drug tests,
        81–82
    and performance-enhancing
        drugs, 75–83
St. John's Wort, 72–73
steroids, 10, 75, 76, 79, 81
stimulants, 8, 10, 14, 15, 16, 62
"Suzie," 7–9, 11
Syria, 19–20

trafficking, drug, 24, 27, **37**, 39–41
    See also crime
tranquilizers, 8, 21, 44, 61, 62
treatments, drug. *See* rehabilitation,
    drug addiction
Turing Pharmaceuticals, 66–67

United Nations Drug Control
    Program (UNDCP), 24, 26, 27,
    28, 31
United Nations Office on Drugs
    and Crime (UNODC), 20–21

vaccines, 58–60, 86
    See also medicinal drugs
Valium, 10, 62

"war on drugs," 45–46, 95, 96–97
    See also crime
Wilkinson, Francis, 47–48
withdrawal symptoms, 34, 38,
    61–62
World Anti-Doping Agency, 81–82
World Health Organization
    (WHO), **60**, 64, 70, 90

Xanax, 10, 62

About the Author

Jon Reese lives in Birmingham, Alabama, with his wife Kate and their five children. After graduating from the University of Tennesse, he has worked for twenty-six years as an elementary school gym teacher. This is his first book for young people.